STRIP
your stash

DYNAMIC QUILTS MADE FROM STRIPS

12 Projects in Multiple Sizes from GE Designs

GUDRUN ERLA

stashBOOKS.
an imprint of C&T Publishing

Library of Congress Cataloging-in-Publication Data

Erla, Gudrun.

Strip your stash : dynamic quilts made from strips : 12 projects in multiple
sizes from GE designs / Gudrun Erla.

     pages cm

ISBN 978-1-60705-740-6 (soft cover)

1. Patchwork quilts. 2. Quilting--Patterns. 3. Strip quilting--Patterns.
I. Title.

TT835.E76 2015

746.46--dc23

                                        2014048648

Printed in China

10 9 8 7 6 5 4 3 2 1

Contents

Acknowledgments

As much fun as I had working on the quilts in this book and getting all things written and handed in on time, I would never have finished without the help of some fantastic people in my life.

My kids Atli, Gisli, and Svana: You are my biggest supporters and inspiration at the same time. Thanks for understanding when I am deep in a project and don't respond.

My assistant Yvonne Geske, thank you for always being there for me, whether it is helping with sewing, processing orders, or just keeping me sane with our laughs and deep talks.

Thank you to my wonderful longarm quilters Harriet Bollig, Angela Walters, and Teresa Silva. Without you, these quilts would be just bleh.

Thank you to Lissa Alexander and Moda Fabrics, Alex Veronelli and Aurifil, and the people at Creative Grids, for providing fabric, thread, and wonderful rulers for the quilts in the book.

And finally, thank you to my wonderful book team at Stash Books: Gailen, Roxane, Michele, Alison, Katie V.A., Freesia, April, Katie M., Kristy, Debbie, Nissa, Diane, Mary Peyton, and Tim.

Introduction

I have been collecting strips ever since I had the privilege of taking a class with one of my quilting idols, Debbie Caffrey, shortly after I started quilting. She told us to cut up our leftover yardage into 2½˝ strips and store them that way, ready to go for the next project. I knew from experience that when I had 4˝–6˝ of fabric folded and stored in my cabinets, they would easily get lost in the stack of fabric, and I rarely ever used them up. When I did decide to use that fabric, I first had to iron it and then cut it up. So, of course, I took in every word Debbie said and have been storing my strips in color-coordinated drawers for years. This practice started way before precut strips were available for quilters. Over the years, my drawers of strips have grown to include left-over strips from jelly rolls that I didn't use in certain projects. These drawers are a great treasure in my sewing room. I go to them all the time, whether I am testing out a new strip pattern concept, looking to make a quick quilt for a gift, or even working on a new project for a book. Something about pulling out the fabric needed for a quilt, already cut into strips and ready to go, is so fulfilling! The collection also gives me the variety of colors, textures, and depth that is hard to find when I try to work from just a single collection.

This book includes twelve quilts that are all made using 2½˝ strips—known as Jelly Rolls, Roll-Ups, Bali Pops, Tonga Treats, and many other names—and a few coordinating fabrics. Many of the quilts were made from my eclectic drawers of strips. Others come from an already-coordinated collection of strips from the quilt shop. I hope the different options and styles will give you the inspiration to take whichever route you prefer to follow when making these fresh, original quilts to your exact style.

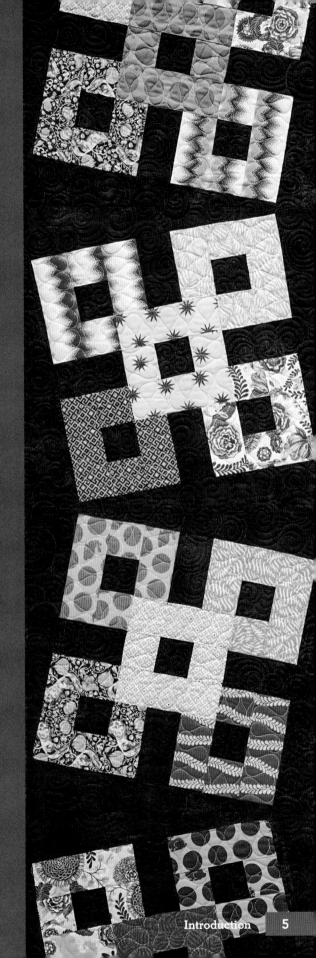

stripping

Many quilters think that making scrappy quilts means giving up total control and grabbing the next fabric piece. That kind of "fly by the seat of your pants" method is not really necessary in most cases; you can plan out your quilt and make it look scrappy at the same time.

When choosing strips and coordinating fabrics for your quilt, start with the quilt design. Some patterns call for a more controlled colorway, while others benefit from throwing some unexpected colors and fabric designs into the mix for extra interest. Here are some tips for stripping and picking fabrics that give a little insight into my choices.

Collecting and Storing Your Strips

Whenever I have yardage in less than a ¼ yard, I always cut it into 2½˝-wide strips. These days a vast collection of coordinated strip packs is also available in quilt shops. The different fabric companies call them different names—Jelly Rolls, Roll-Ups, Bali Pops, Tonga Treats—but they are all pretty much the same thing—a collection of 2½˝ strips from a single fabric line. The precut packets are a great way to start a collection of strips or to grab for use in an already-coordinated quilt.

If you feel your strip stash needs more variety, there are many ways to do that economically. Round up your quilting friends and organize a "strip swap." Get four quilter friends. Cut four identical strips of six different fabrics, which totals about 1¾ yards. Meet with your friends and trade strips so that each person in the swap receives six different strips from four different people. You go home with 24 different strips. Choose themes for each swap—holiday fabric, batiks, florals, basics, and so on. Swaps like this could be done on a larger scale, within quilt guilds, in classes, or at your local quilt shop.

I like to organize my strips by color. I store them in clear plastic drawers that measure 12˝ × 9˝ and 2¾˝ deep. A strip cut from the full width of the fabric folded in half twice fits perfectly. Mostly I save full width-of-fabric strips. But sometimes I save two half-strips of the same fabric, because I may be able to use it as one strip in a pattern, which is a great option for leftover fat-quarter pieces.

I lay my strips vertically in the drawers, with the folded edge to the front, which makes it easier to see what I have so I can pull out just the right color strip.

PREPARING YOUR STRIPS

I never prewash my fabrics, and so far I have not had any issues with dye running when I do wash my quilts. If you buy precut strip packets, they certainly should not be prewashed, because they will end up a tangled mess and not the same size as when they went in the machine. When I get a strip packet or jelly roll, I always start by pressing my strips with a little steam, being careful not to distort them. Pressing the strips takes care of most of the shrinkage, if any. Make sure to press the center crease out if your pattern requires making full width of fabric strip units. After pressing, I measure the strips to make sure that they are 2½˝ wide.

Some companies have pinked strips, and the pinking can be different sizes. Therefore, I recommend measuring strips; if the pinking makes the strip a little bit wider then 2½˝, trim it to 2½˝ right away for more accurate piecing.

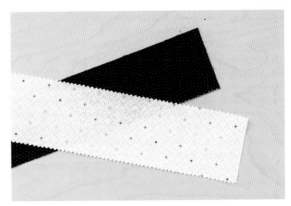

Example of a pinked-edge strip versus a straight-edge strip

BACKGROUND FABRICS

The choice of background will sometimes make the most difference in a quilt's overall look and feel. Make sure to try your strips on different backgrounds with different colors and textures. You never know what will really make the strips pop until you try it.

Some of my favorite backgrounds have a little bit of a tone-on-tone print or a texture.

My favorite choices for backgrounds are tone-on-tones and textured prints. Solids also work well as backgrounds because they will give your quilt a flatter overall look and sometimes a vintage feel, especially when you mix them with prints. I do use neutral colors quite a bit, ranging from white to black and any shade of gray in between. Although the neutrals will not fight with the other colors, it is still important to try them together.

Here is an example: I thought I had the perfect background for my *Feathers* quilt all picked out and ready before I started sewing. But once I had finished the strip units and started laying out the quilt with the background, I realized that the gray was too light for my strips to really stand out and shine. I tried another darker background that I had, but that one didn't work either because there was too much black in it. Third try was the charm with the perfect shade of gray. Yes, there really are much more than 50 shades of gray in the world. ☺

Trying a few different shades of background fabric will help you make the best choice.

QUILTS WITH A CONTROLLED COLORWAY

A few of the quilts in this book are put together with a controlled colorway, which is where I choose one or two colors and pull strips in those colors to pull the complete look together.

Jelly Forest

I obviously wanted my trees for *Jelly Forest* (page 18) to be green, but I also needed them to have a variety of greens to give them some interest. I wanted them to go from a bright lime green to a deep forest green without going too much overboard. I also wanted the strips to have different textures and different-sized patterns. I tried to stay with tone-on-tone prints because I wanted the trees to look sleek and modern. A pattern with other colors in it would not have helped with that.

I pulled out tone-on-tone strips in various shades of green, making sure I had a good range of colors, from light lime green to dark forest green, that all played well together. After looking at them closely, I removed two of the strips; one was too light and came off as solid, and the other one was a different shade of green that didn't mesh with the others.

Dreamweaver

Dreamweaver (page 26) is based on using two colors of strips, along with a background and an accent fabric. I chose orange and green on a gray background with a light cream accent.

Feathers

My fabric choice for *Feathers* (page 34) was based on a shopping trip while teaching in Colorado. I had picked up a collection of fat quarters in these gorgeous reds and golds on a white background that I really wanted to use, but I felt like I needed to add some more gold and red to them to tie it all together.

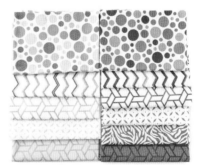

Sometimes a coordinated purchase from a quilt shop will inspire the look of a quilt. It is good to be able to supplement it with your precut strip stash. The polka dot fabrics helped me choose the red and yellow coordinating strips in the various shades.

QUILTS WITH DISTINCT BLOCKS

Some of the quilts in this book have blocks that need contrast for them to really shine.

Pixie Stix

The block for *Pixie Stix* (page 42) consists of four different-colored "stix" that overlap each other. For the block to really come to life, those four colors needed to contrast enough to stand out from the others. The background also needed to be a good contrast to the strips in order to achieve the desired look.

Casanova

A little bit of planning is involved in *Casanova* (page 52) if you want a look similar to what I did. I wanted each block to have four different colors, and I wanted those colors bright and bold to make the quilt sharp. Most times I like to mix different fabric lines together in a quilt, just to get more variety in the prints and shapes. In this case, however, I found two fabric lines from Moda that had a very similar color story and that mixed well together. "Best. Day. Ever!" by April Rosenthal has a modern/retro feel, and "Fancy" by Lily Ashbury really rounded out the assortment with some classic style.

Mixing fabric lines together, even if you are working from precut strip packets like jelly rolls, gives your quilt more depth, with greater variety in the fabric patterns and subtle shade differences in the color.

Square Dance

The block for *Square Dance* (page 60) has cuts from five different strips to make the squares. For the block to be successful, the strips need to have some contrast with each other. It is okay if the strip fabrics have some pattern and various colors within them, as long as the background fabric is a good contrast to them all and makes the block shine. I mainly used Tula Pink's "Fox Field" fabric line for the strips; the navy blue grunge fabric from Moda was the perfect background.

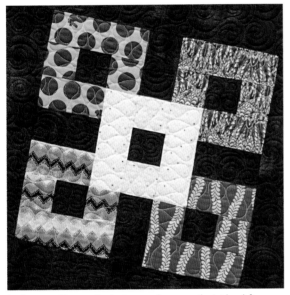

In *Square Dance*, I tried to make sure that I had five colors in each block. When that wasn't possible, I placed the similar colors opposite each other so they wouldn't interrupt the design.

Ripple Effect

Ripple Effect (page 68) doesn't really need much color planning for the block since one strip makes one block. However, I wanted to include it here because not all fabrics will show off the block perfectly. I tried to use mostly tone-on-tone prints and then mixed smaller prints with more color in between.

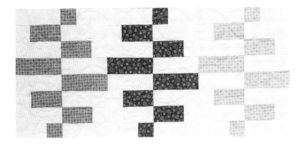

Ribbon Candy

With two shades of the same color in each block, *Ribbon Candy* (page 74) gets the right feel and look, weaving together the light and dark shade of the same color.

QUILTS FOR THE SCRAP CRAZIES

The four remaining quilts I haven't mentioned are quilts for the true scrappies. Yes, you! ☺ If you like to just grab strips and go, these are for you. These quilts will shine in an array of scrappy fabric choices, with the perfect choice of background or accent fabric helping to make them sing.

Pebbles

Pebbles (page 82) is a perfect choice for using a variety of scrappy strips. I fell in love with the colorway of the "Persimmon" fabric line by BasicGrey for Moda, with its blues, grays, mustards, and burnt oranges. Then I saw the "Modern Neutrals" line by Amy Ellis; it had a very similar color story but a more modern style. I love mixing the two—modern and traditional—any way I can. In this quilt, they came together perfectly.

Two different fabric lines by two different designers came together in perfect harmony in *Pebbles*.

Pixel Wheels

The amount of background versus strips used in *Pixel Wheels* (page 88) is quite overwhelming. Therefore, it is important to choose strips that really stand out from the background to make each little square count once it is in the design.

I chose to use some of my Kate Spain stash for this quilt, with one of my own fabrics as a background.

Bob and Weave

Bob and Weave (page 94) has a very modern feel to it, so I wanted to use some unconventional fabrics for it. I fell in love with Katarina Roccella's "Indelible" line for Art Gallery Fabrics and its colors. It's very forward and unusual but gorgeous at the same time. It is probably not a fabric that makes you want to cut it up into strips, because of some of the gorgeous large-scale prints. But that is exactly why I chose to use the line. If you are going for unconventional, go all in!

Hang Glide

The strip portion of *Hang Glide* (page 102) really melds together in a strippy bliss, and the design comes through with the accent fabric choices. I have been hoarding a collection of low-volume strips with some of my favorite typography and other fabrics, and I knew this was the perfect project to break them out. I chose some standout color accents to really contrast the low-volume blocks and tie the quilt together. This quilt would also look great with the color stories reversed, with crazy colors in the strip portion and more neutrals in the accents. Whichever way you chose, this quilt is sure to satisfy the true scrappies.

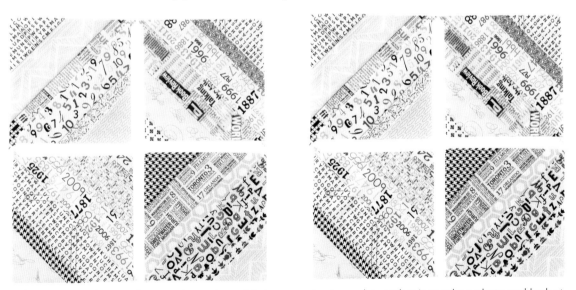

A fast way to make sure that your low-volume fabrics are going to work together is to take a photo and look at it from a distance or even convert the photo into black and white. The image will show you right away whether any of the fabrics stand out too much from the others.

General Instructions

Be sure to read all instructions completely before beginning a project. The preparations for the different projects in this book might differ a little bit. A good rule is to read through each step before beginning that step. For best results, always choose quilt shop–quality 100% cotton fabrics for your projects.

SEWING

Use a scant ¼″ seam allowance for all projects unless otherwise stated. Check the accuracy of your seam allowance before you begin; make adjustments if needed.

PRESSING

Use a light steam if possible when pressing. If you don't have a steam iron, use a hot iron and have a spray bottle with water handy if needed. Press in the direction described in the text or follow the arrows when they are shown.

BORDERS

Sew all your border strips diagonally together into one long strip (unless they were cut lengthwise). Measure the length of your quilt on each side and through the center. Find the median of measurements and cut borders from the long strip to that length. Then sew them on each side. Press. Repeat the process for the top and bottom borders, measuring across the width of the quilt top.

QUILTING

All of the quilts in this book were machine quilted on a longarm quilting machine, but hand quilting is, of course, possible with all projects, as is using a domestic machine.

BINDING

I prefer to use a double-folded binding technique for my quilts.

Straight-grain binding

Cut your binding strips 2½″ wide across the width of fabric on the straight of grain. Diagonally piece the binding strips together and trim the seam allowance to ¼″. Press seams open. Fold the strip in half lengthwise, wrong sides together, and press.

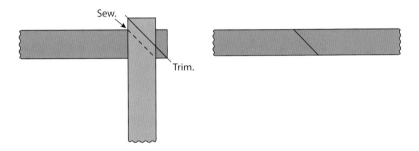

With raw edges of the binding and quilt top together, pin and stitch the binding to the quilt, starting a few inches away from a corner, leaving the first 8″ of the binding unattached. Miter the binding at the corners by folding the binding up and away from the quilt (so the raw edges make a straight line) and then folding it down, so it is even with the quilt's raw edge.

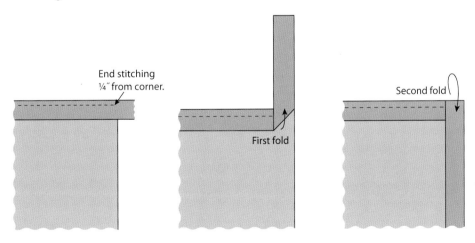

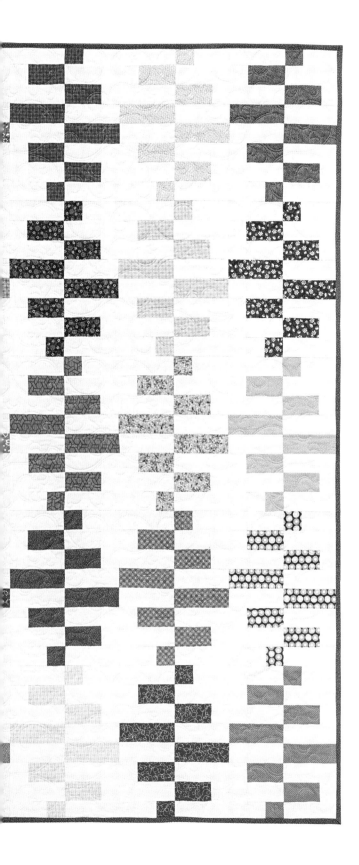

Continue sewing binding all the way around the quilt, stopping about 10″ from the starting point. Lay the end of the binding over the beginning and trim so that they overlap by 2½″. Unfold the ends and bring them together at a 90° angle, right sides together. Sew them together on the diagonal, trim the seam allowance to ¼″, and press the seam open. Fold the binding in half again and finish sewing it to the quilt. Fold the binding over the raw edges to the back of the quilt and sew the binding in place.

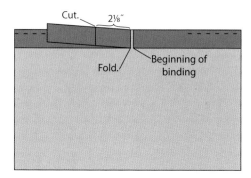

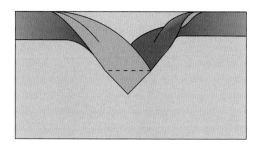

CONTROLLED COLORWAY

Jelly Forest

Finished block: 15″ × 15″ • **Quilt sizes:** lap, full

Materials

MATERIALS	LAP SIZE 54¾″ × 80¼″	FULL SIZE 86¼″ × 86¼″
2½″ × WOF* STRIPS	18	29
BACKGROUND FABRIC	2 yards	3 yards
TRUNK/BORDER FABRIC	2 yards	3¼ yards
BINDING	⅝ yard	¾ yard
BACKING	5 yards	8 yards
BATTING	63″ × 88″	94″ × 94″

WOF = width of fabric

Yardage based on 42″ width of fabric.

Cutting

MATERIALS	LAP SIZE 8 BLOCKS	FULL SIZE 13 BLOCKS
2½″ × WOF STRIPS	Cut the following rectangles from the assorted strips:	
2½″ × 15½″	8	13
2½″ × 13½″	8	13
2½″ × 12½″	8	13
2½″ × 10½″	8	13
2½″ × 9½″	8	13
2½″ × 7½″	8	13
2½″ × 6½″	8	13
2½″ × 4½″	8	13
2½″ × 3½″	8	13
2½″ × 1½″	8	13

CUTTING continued on next page

MATERIALS	LAP SIZE 8 BLOCKS	FULL SIZE 13 BLOCKS
BACKGROUND FABRIC		
Cut strips 1½˝ × WOF.	14	23
Subcut into rectangles:		
1½˝ × 13½˝	8	13
1½˝ × 12½˝	8	13
1½˝ × 10½˝	8	13
1½˝ × 9½˝	8	13
1½˝ × 7½˝	8	13
1½˝ × 6½˝	8	13
1½˝ × 4½˝	8	13
1½˝ × 3½˝	8	13
Subcut into squares:		
1½˝ × 1½˝	8	13
Cut strips 3½˝ × WOF.	12	18
Subcut into:		
3½˝ × 15½˝ rectangles	24	36
3½˝ × 3½˝ squares	1	2
TRUNK/BORDER FABRIC		
Cut strips 3½˝ × WOF.	3	5
Subcut into 3½˝ × 3½˝ squares.	34	56
Cut 18¼˝ × 18¼˝ squares. **Cut each twice diagonally to make side setting triangles.**	2 (8 triangles; you will use 6)	2 (8 triangles)
Cut 7¼˝ × 7¼˝ squares. **Cut each once diagonally to make corner setting triangles.**	2 (4 triangles)	2 (4 triangles)
Cut strips 4½˝ × WOF for borders.	7	
Cut strips 7½˝ × WOF for borders.		9
BINDING		
Cut strips 2½˝ × WOF.	8	9

Jelly Forest, lap size. Sewn by Gudrun Erla, quilted by Harriet Bollig.

Construction

Seam allowances are ¼˝.

BLOCK ASSEMBLY

Follow the arrows for pressing direction.

Make the blocks

1. Sew a 1½˝ × 1½˝ background square to a 2½˝ × 1½˝ green rectangle. Press. `Figure A`

A

2. Sew a green 2½˝ × 3½˝ rectangle to the left of the Step 1 unit. Press. `Figure B`

B

3. Sew a 1½˝ × 3½˝ background rectangle to the bottom of the Step 2 unit. Press. `Figure C`

C

4. Sew a 1½˝ × 4½˝ background rectangle to the left of the Step 3 unit. Press. `Figure D`

D

5. Sew a 2½˝ × 4½˝ green rectangle to the bottom of the Step 4 unit. Press. Then add a 2½˝ × 6½˝ green rectangle to the left of the unit and press. `Figure E`

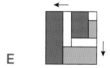
E

6. Sew a 1½˝ × 6½˝ background rectangle to the bottom of the Step 5 unit. Press. Then add a 1½˝ × 7½˝ background rectangle to the left of the unit and press. `Figure F`

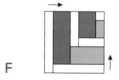
F

7. Sew a 2½˝ × 7½˝ green rectangle to the bottom of the Step 6 unit. Press. Then add a 2½˝ × 9½˝ green rectangle to the left of the unit and press. `Figure G`

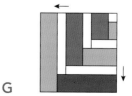
G

8. Keep adding longer rectangles to the block as before, alternating background and green, pressing after each seam until you have added the 2½˝ × 15½˝ green rectangle. **Figure H**

9. Repeat Steps 1–8 to make 8 blocks for lap size or 13 blocks for full size.

Make the sashing units

1. Draw a diagonal line on the wrong side of all the trunk 3½˝ × 3½˝ squares. **Figure I**

2. Layer a trunk square on each end of a 3½˝ × 15½˝ background rectangle. Make sure to orient the diagonal line exactly as shown. Sew on the drawn line, trim the seam allowance to ¼˝, and press. Repeat this step to make 4 sashing strips and 4 mirror-image sashing strips for lap size or 8 sashing strips and 8 mirror-image sashing strips for full size. **Figure J**

3. Layer a trunk square on the left side of a 3½˝ × 15½˝ background rectangle. Make sure to orient the diagonal line exactly as shown. Sew on the drawn line, trim the seam allowance to ¼˝, and press. Repeat this step to make 6 sashing strips and 6 mirror-image sashing strips for lap size or 7 sashing strips and 7 mirror-image sashing strips for full size. **Figure K**

H

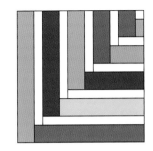

I

J

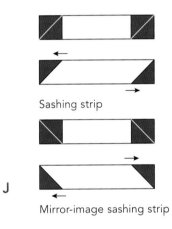

Sashing strip

Mirror-image sashing strip

K

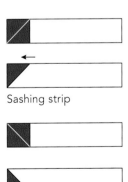

Sashing strip

Mirror-image sashing strip

QUILT ASSEMBLY

1. Arrange the blocks on point, with the sashing strips and background and remaining trunk 3½˝ × 3½˝ squares as shown, to make the trees and trunks. Place the large setting triangles on the sides.

Lap: 3 columns of 3 and 2 blocks (Refer to the row assembly diagram, at right.)

Full: 5 columns of 3 and 2 blocks (Refer to the quilt assembly diagram, page 25.)

---

2. Sew the blocks and sashing strips together into diagonal rows as shown. Make sure to align the large triangles with the inside edges of the rows. Sew the 3½˝ × 3½˝ squares and sashing strips into rows. Press all the seams toward the sashing strips.

3. Sew the rows together, matching the seam intersections in sashing rows and block rows. Use a long ruler to square up all 4 sides of the quilt top, allowing ¼˝ for seam allowances so that the tree blocks and trunks will have perfect points.

4. Sew the small corner triangles to all 4 corners of the quilt and press outward.

Row assembly, lap size

BORDERS

Sew the 4½″-wide (lap) or 7½″-wide (full) border strips together into a long strip and attach the border to the quilt. (See Borders, page 14.)

Quilt assembly, lap size

Quilt assembly, full size

FINISHING

1. Layer the top, batting, and backing and quilt as desired.

2. Add the binding. (See General Instructions, page 14.)

Dreamweaver

Finished block: 10˝ × 10˝ • **Quilt sizes:** crib, lap, twin, full, queen

Materials

MATERIALS	CRIB SIZE 40″ × 60″	LAP SIZE 60″ × 80″	TWIN SIZE 60″ × 90″	FULL SIZE 80″ × 90″	QUEEN SIZE 90″ × 100″
2½″ × WOF* STRIPS, COLOR 1	8	16	18	24	30
2½″ × WOF STRIPS, COLOR 2	8	16	18	24	30
BACKGROUND FABRIC	1¼ yards	2½ yards	3 yards	3⅝ yards	4¾ yards
ACCENT FABRIC	⅓ yard	½ yard	⅝ yard	¾ yard	1 yard
BINDING FABRIC	½ yard	⅝ yard	⅝ yard	¾ yard	⅞ yard
BACKING FABRIC	2⅞ yards	5 yards	5⅝ yards	7½ yards	8⅓ yards
BATTING	48″ × 68″	68″ × 88″	68″ × 98″	88″ × 98″	98″ × 108″

* WOF = width of fabric

Yardage based on 42″ width of fabric.

Cutting

MATERIALS	CRIB SIZE 24 BLOCKS	LAP SIZE 48 BLOCKS	TWIN SIZE 54 BLOCKS	FULL SIZE 72 BLOCKS	QUEEN SIZE 90 BLOCKS
2½˝ × WOF STRIPS, COLOR 1	Cut the following rectangles from each strip:				
2½˝ × 8½˝	3*	3*	3*	3*	3*
2½˝ × WOF STRIPS, COLOR 2	Cut the following rectangles from each strip:				
2½˝ × 8½˝	3*	3*	3*	3*	3*
BACKGROUND FABRIC					
Cut strips 4½˝ × WOF.	3	6	7	9	12
Cut strips 2½˝ × WOF.	11	22	25	33	42
Subcut into: 2½˝ × 16½˝ rectangles	16	32	36	48	60
2½˝ × 2½˝ squares	72	144	162	216	270
ACCENT FABRIC					
Cut strips 2½˝ × WOF.	3	6	7	9	12
BINDING FABRIC					
Cut strips 2½˝ × WOF.	6	8	8	9	10

* Save the rest of the strip for strip piecing.

Dreamweaver, lap size. Sewn by Gudrun Erla, quilted by Angela Walters.

Construction

Seam allowances are ¼″.

BLOCK ASSEMBLY

Follow the arrows for pressing direction. For each block, work with all color 1 pieces of the same fabric, and all color 2 pieces of the same fabric. Figure A

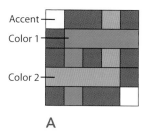

A

Make the blocks

1. Sew a 2½″ × 2½″ background square to each 2½″ × 8½″ color 1 and color 2 rectangle. Press. Figure B

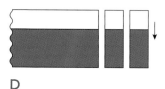

B

2. Sew a 2½″ × 16½″ background rectangle to each leftover color 1 and color 2 strip to make strip sets. Press. Cut 6 units 2½″ wide from each strip set. Figure C

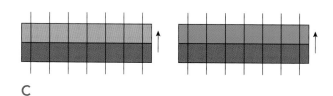

C

3. Sew a 2½″-wide accent strip to a 4½″-wide background strip. Press. Repeat this step to make 3 strip sets for crib size, 6 for lap size, 7 for twin size, 9 for full size, or 12 for queen size. Subcut the units into 2½″-wide units. You will need 48 for crib size, 96 for lap size, 108 for twin size, 144 for full size, or 180 for queen size. Figure D

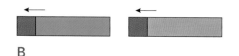

D

4. For each block you will need 1 of each color 1 and color 2 unit from Step 1, 2 each of the color 1 and color 2 Step 2 units, 2 Step 3 units, and a 2½″ × 2½″ background square. Use all color 1 pieces from 1 fabric and color 2 pieces from 1 fabric in a block.

5. Sew the 2½″ × 2½″ background square between a color 1 and color 2 unit from Step 2, oriented as shown. Press. **Figure E**

6. Sew a color 1 unit from Step 2 to a unit from Step 3 as shown; press. Sew a color 2 unit to the other Step 3 unit as shown and press. **Figure F**

7. Arrange the block in rows, using the unit from Step 5 in the center, then the color 1 and color 2 units from Step 1, and finally the Step 6 units. Rotate the units as needed to orient them as shown. Sew the rows together. Press all the seams away from the center unit. **Figure G**

8. Repeat Steps 4–7 to make 24 blocks for crib size, 48 for lap size, 54 for twin size, 72 for full size, or 90 for queen size.

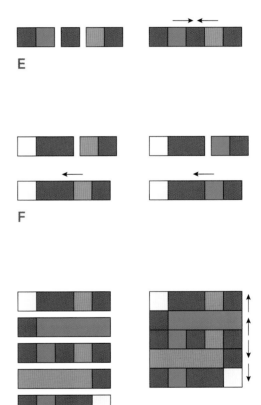

E

F

G

QUILT ASSEMBLY

1. Refer to the quilt assembly diagram (page 33). Arrange the blocks into rows according to the size you are making, rotating the blocks so the color 1 and color 2 strips align as shown:

Crib: 6 rows of 4 blocks

Lap: 8 rows of 6 blocks

Twin: 9 rows of 6 blocks

Full: 9 rows of 8 blocks.

Queen: 10 rows of 9 blocks

2. Sew the blocks together into rows. Press the seams in row 1 to the right, row 2 to the left, and so on.

3. Sew the rows together and press.

FINISHING

1. Layer the top, batting, and backing and quilt as desired.

2. Add the binding. (See General Instructions, page 14.)

Quilt assembly, lap size

Feathers

Quilt sizes: lap, twin, full

Materials

MATERIALS	LAP SIZE 47″ × 56¾″	TWIN SIZE 62″ × 96¼″	FULL SIZE 77″ × 96¼″
2½″ × WOF* STRIPS	20	40	52
BACKGROUND FABRIC	1½ yards	3¼ yards	4 yards
BINDING FABRIC	½ yard	⅝ yard	¾ yard
BACKING FABRIC	3¼ yards	5⅜ yards	5⅜ yards**
BATTING	55″ × 65″	70″ × 104″	85″ × 104″

* WOF = width of fabric

Yardage based on 42″ width of fabric.

** *Exception: Full size backing requires 44″ usable width of fabric or additional yardage to piece.*

Cutting

MATERIALS	LAP SIZE 9 BLOCKS	TWIN SIZE 20 BLOCKS	FULL SIZE 25 BLOCKS
BACKGROUND FABRIC			
Cut strips 6½″ × WOF.	3	8	10
Subcut into 6½″-wide 45° diamonds.	12	32	40
Cut strips 7″ × WOF	1	2	2
Subcut into 7″ × 7″ squares. Cut each once diagonally.	6 (12 triangles)	8 (16 triangles)	10 (20 triangles)
Cut strips 1½″ × WOF.	5	10	12
Cut strips 2½″ × WOF.	6	12	15
BINDING FABRIC			
Cut strips 2½″ × WOF.	6	9	9

Feathers, twin size. Sewn by Gudrun Erla, quilted by Harriet Bollig.

Construction

Seam allowances are ¼˝.

BLOCK ASSEMBLY

Follow the arrows for pressing direction.

Make the strip sets

1. If you are making either the lap size or the full size quilt, cut 4 of the assorted 2½˝ × width of fabric strips in half on the fold so they measure about 21˝, because you will be making some half strip sets.

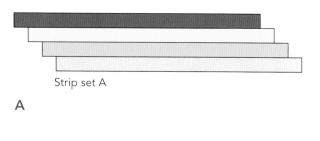

Strip set A

A

Make strip set A by sewing together 4 of the assorted 2½˝ × width of fabric strips, staggering them 2˝ apart as shown. Press the seams in 1 direction. Make 2 full strip sets and 1 half strip set for lap size, 5 for twin size, or 6 full and 1 half for full size. **Figure A**

2. Subcut the units into 6½˝ diamonds as shown. Lay a long ruler on top of the strip unit, aligning the 45° degree line on the ruler along an edge of the strip set. Make the first cut to get that 45° edge on the strip set. Then align the 6½˝ line on the ruler along that first diagonal cut and cut 4 A diamonds from each strip set. You will need 9 for lap size, 20 for twin size, or 25 for full size. **Figure B**

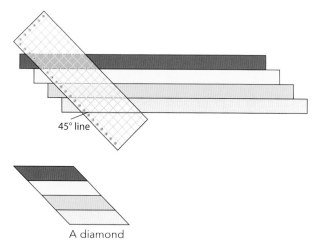

45° line

A diamond

B

3. Make strip set B by sewing together 4 of the assorted 2½˝ × width of fabric strips, staggering them 2˝ apart as shown, which is the opposite of the A strip sets. Press the seams in 1 direction. Make 2 full strip sets and 1 half strip set for lap size, 5 for twin size, or 6 full and 1 half for full size. **Figure C**

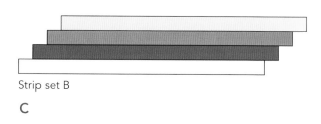

Strip set B

C

4. Subcut the B strip sets into 6½″ diamonds as in Step 2, but these should be the mirror image of the A diamonds. Cut 4 B diamonds from each strip set. You will need 9 for lap size, 20 for twin size, or 25 for full size. **Figure D**

QUILT ASSEMBLY

1. Arrange the A and B diamond blocks and the background diamonds and triangles into pairs of columns as shown, alternating the direction in which the diamonds point in each pair, according to the size you are making:

> **Lap:** 3 pairs of columns (A and B) of 3 diamond blocks
>
> **Twin:** 4 pairs of columns each of 5 diamond blocks
>
> **Full:** 5 pairs of columns each of 5 diamond blocks

Figure E

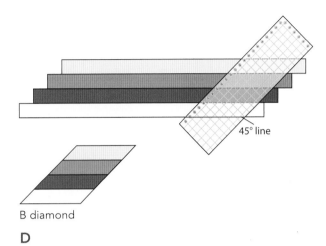

B diamond

D

Column assembly, twin or full size

E

2. Sew the blocks and diamonds together into columns. Sew a background triangle to each end. When sewing the diamonds together, make sure to align the seam intersections. Press the seams toward the background fabric. **Figure F**

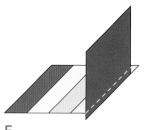

F

3. Sew all the 1½˝ background strips into a long strip and press the seams open. Cut 3 sashing strips 56¾˝ long for lap size, 4 strips 96¼˝ long for twin size, or 5 strips 96¼˝ long for full size.

4. Repeat Step 3 with all of the 2½˝ background strips. Cut 4 sashing strips 56¾˝ long for lap size, 5 strips 96¼˝ long for twin size, or 6 strips 96¼˝ long for full size.

5. Arrange the 1½˝ strips between the A and B columns that are pointing in the same direction. Add the 2½˝ sashing strips between the remaining columns and on each end as shown. Sew the columns and sashing strips together and press toward the sashing. Trim the quilt top to square up if needed. **Figure F**

FINISHING

1. Layer the top, batting, and backing and quilt as desired.

2. Add the binding. (See General Instructions, page 14.)

Quilt assembly, twin size

G

DISTINCT BLOCKS

Pixie Stix

Finished block: 14″ × 14″ • **Quilt sizes:** crib, lap, twin, queen

Materials

MATERIALS	CRIB SIZE 44″ × 58″	LAP SIZE 58″ × 86″	TWIN SIZE 72″ × 86″	QUEEN SIZE 86″ × 100″
2½″ × WOF* STRIPS	8	20	27	40
BACKGROUND FABRIC	2¼ yards	4 yards	5 yards	6½ yards
BINDING FABRIC	½ yard	⅝ yard	¾ yard	⅞ yard
BACKING FABRIC	3 yards	5⅝ yards	6⅞ yards	8 yards
BATTING	52″ × 66″	66″ × 94″	80″ × 94″	94″ × 108″

* WOF = width of fabric

Yardage based on 42″ width of fabric.

Cutting

MATERIALS	CRIB SIZE 6 BLOCKS	LAP SIZE 15 BLOCKS	TWIN SIZE 20 BLOCKS	QUEEN SIZE 30 BLOCKS
2½˝ × WOF STRIPS	From each strip, cut 3 rectangles 2½˝ × 6½˝; put the rest of the strip (about 20˝ long) aside for strip piecing.			
BACKGROUND FABRIC				
Cut strips 2½˝ × WOF.	5	11	14	21
Subcut into: 2½˝ × 6½˝ rectangles 2½˝ × 2½˝ squares	24 6	60 15	80 20	120 30
Cut strips 2½˝ × WOF.	8	20	27	40
Subcut each strip on the fold so it measures about 20˝ long.				
Cut strips 3½˝ × WOF for borders.	9	14	16	18
Cut strips 2½˝ × WOF for pieced border.	4	4	4	4
BINDING FABRIC				
Cut strips 2½˝ × WOF.	6	8	9	10

Pixie Stix, lap size. Sewn by Gudrun Erla, quilted by Rita Kroening.

Construction

Seam allowances are ¼˝.

BLOCK ASSEMBLY

Follow the arrows for pressing direction.

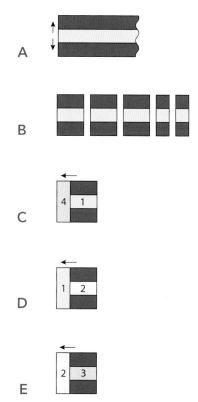

A

B

C

D

E

Make the strip sets

1. Sew a 2½˝ × 20˝ light strip between 2 background 2½˝ × 20˝ strips. Press toward the background fabric. Repeat this step to make 8 strip sets for crib size, 20 for lap size, 27 for twin size, or 40 for queen size.
Figure A

2. Cut each of the strip sets from Step 1 into 3 units 4½˝ wide. For crib size only, cut 2 units 2½˝ wide from each remaining strip set. For all other quilt sizes, cut 1 unit 2½˝ wide from each strip set. Group the units with the same fabrics together to stay organized. **Figure B**

Make the blocks

1. Choose 4 different 4½˝-wide strip set units. Find 4 matching 2˝ × 6½˝ rectangles. Assign each color a number from 1 to 4.

2. Sew a color 4 rectangle to a color 1 strip set unit as shown. Press. **Figure C**

3. Sew a color 1 rectangle to a color 2 strip set unit as shown. Press. **Figure D**

4. Sew a color 2 rectangle to a color 3 strip set unit as shown. Press. **Figure E**

5. Sew a color 3 rectangle to a color 4 strip set unit as shown. Press. **Figure F**

F

6. Sew a 2″ × 6½″ background rectangle to each unit from Steps 2–5. Press. **Figure G**

G

7. Begin to sew the 4 units from Step 6 together, along with a 2½″ × 2½″ background square, using a partial seam method. Place the background square, right sides together, on the bottom right corner of unit 1/2. Start the seam in the middle of the square and sew down to the edge of the square as shown. Press. **Figure H**

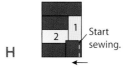

H

8. Now sew unit 4/1 below the first unit. Press. **Figure I**

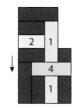

I

9. Sew unit 3/4 to the right-hand side of the second unit and press. **Figure J**

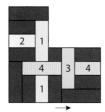

J

10. Fold down the first unit to better access the seam. Sew unit 2/3 above the third unit. Press. **Figure K**

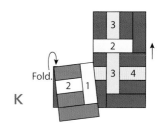

K

11. Fold the first unit toward the center to line up the raw edges. Finish that first seam all the way. Press. Your block should measure 14½″ × 14½″ unfinished. **Figure L**

12. Repeat Steps 1–11 to make 6 blocks for crib size, 15 for lap size, 20 for twin size, or 30 for queen size.

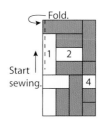

QUILT ASSEMBLY

1. Refer to the quilt assembly diagram (page 51) to arrange the blocks into rows according to the size you are making:

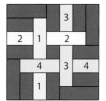

L

> **Crib:** 3 rows of 2 blocks
>
> **Lap:** 5 rows of 3 blocks
>
> **Twin:** 5 rows of 4 blocks
>
> **Queen:** 6 rows of 5 blocks

2. Sew the blocks together into rows. Press the seams in row 1 to the right, row 2 to the left, and so on.

3. Sew the rows together and press.

BORDER ASSEMBLY

1. Sew the 3½˝ background strips diagonally together into a long strip and attach it to the quilt. (See Borders, page 14.)

2. Sew the 2½˝-wide strip set units together at the short ends to make pieced border strips for the quilt size you are making. Press all the seams in the same direction. *You will have some units left over.*

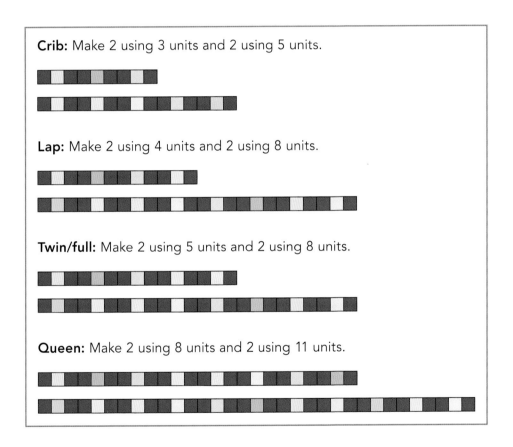

Crib: Make 2 using 3 units and 2 using 5 units.

Lap: Make 2 using 4 units and 2 using 8 units.

Twin/full: Make 2 using 5 units and 2 using 8 units.

Queen: Make 2 using 8 units and 2 using 11 units.

3. Sew a 2½˝ × width of fabric background strip to a short end of each of the pieced border strips. Press.

4. Measure the length of the quilt top. Trim away the excess background strip so the longer pieced borders are the same length. Sew the borders to the long sides of the quilt, arranging the pieced sections at the top right and bottom left edges of the quilt. Press outward.

5. Measure the width of the quilt top. Trim away the excess background strip so the longer pieced borders are the same length. Sew the borders to the short sides of the quilt, arranging the pieced sections at the top right and bottom left edges of the quilt. Press outward.

6. Add another round of borders using the 3½″ border strips and the technique from Step 1. Press.

FINISHING

1. Layer the top, batting, and backing and quilt as desired.

2. Add the binding. (See General Instructions, page 14.)

Quilt assembly, lap size

Casanova

Finished block: 14″ × 15″ • **Quilt sizes:** crib, lap, twin, full/queen, king

Materials

MATERIALS	CRIB SIZE 42″ × 60″	LAP SIZE 56″ × 75″	TWIN SIZE 70″ × 90″	FULL/QUEEN SIZE 84″ × 90″	KING SIZE 98″ × 105″
2½″ × WOF* STRIPS	24	40	60	72	98
BACKGROUND FABRIC	1¼ yards	2 yards	3 yards	3½ yards	4¾ yards
BINDING FABRIC	½ yard	⅝ yard	¾ yard	¾ yard	⅞ yard
BACKING FABRIC	3 yards	3¾ yards	5⅝ yards	7⅞ yards	9 yards
BATTING	50″ × 68″	64″ × 83″	78″ × 98″	92″ × 98″	106″ × 113″

WOF = width of fabric

Yardage based on 42″ width of fabric.

Cutting

MATERIALS	CRIB SIZE 12 BLOCKS	LAP SIZE 20 BLOCKS	TWIN SIZE 30 BLOCKS	FULL/QUEEN SIZE 36 BLOCKS	KING SIZE 49 BLOCKS
ASSORTED 2½″ × WOF STRIPS FOR A, B, G, H	12	20	30	36	49
Cut each strip into rectangles:		From each strip:			
H: 2½″ × 14½″			1		
G: 2½″ × 11½″			1		
B: 2½″ × 4½″			1		
A: 2½″ × 3½″			1		
ASSORTED 2½″ × WOF STRIPS FOR C, D, E, F	12	20	30	36	49
Cut each strip into rectangles:		From each strip:			
F: 2½″ × 11½″			1		
E, D: 2½″ × 8½″			1 of each		
C: 2½″ × 5½″			1		
BACKGROUND FABRIC					
Cut strips 2½″ × WOF.	1	2	3	3	5
Subcut into 2½″ × 3½″ rectangles.	12	20	30	36	49
Cut strips 1½″ × WOF.	24	40	60	72	98
Subcut into rectangles:					
1½″ × 15½″	12	20	30	36	49
1½″ × 13½″	12	20	30	36	49
1½″ × 12½″	12	20	30	36	49
1½″ × 10½″	12	20	30	36	49
1½″ × 9½″	12	20	30	36	49
1½″ × 7½″	12	20	30	36	49
1½″ × 6½″	12	20	30	36	49
1½″ × 4½″	12	20	30	36	49
BINDING FABRIC					
Cut strips 2½″ × WOF.	6	7	9	9	11

Casanova, lap size. Sewn by Yvonne Geske, quilted by Teresa Silva.

Construction

Seam allowances are ¼˝.

BLOCK ASSEMBLY

Follow the arrows for pressing direction.

Make the blocks

1. For 1 block, choose an A and B piece from the same fabric, a C and D from a second fabric, an E and F from a third fabric, and a G and H from a fourth fabric.

2. Sew the A rectangle to a 2½˝ × 3½˝ background rectangle as shown and press. Then sew the B rectangle above the unit as shown and press. **Figure A**

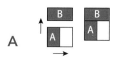

3. Sew a 1½˝ × 4½˝ background rectangle below the unit from Step 2 and press. Then sew a 1½˝ × 6½˝ background rectangle to the right side of the unit and press. **Figure B**

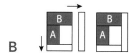

4. Sew the C rectangle below the unit from Step 3 and press. Then sew the D rectangle to the right of the unit and press. **Figure C**

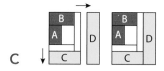

5. Sew a 1½˝ × 7½˝ background rectangle above the unit from Step 4 and press. Then sew a 1½˝ × 9½˝ background rectangle to the left side of the unit and press. **Figure D**

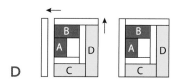

6. Sew the E rectangle above the unit from Step 5 and press. Then sew the F rectangle to the left of the unit and press. **Figure E**

7. Sew a 1½″ × 10½″ background rectangle below the unit from Step 6 and press. Then sew a 1½″ × 12½″ background rectangle to the right side of the unit and press. **Figure F**

8. Sew the G rectangle below the unit from Step 7 and press. Then sew the H rectangle to the right of the unit and press. **Figure G**

9. Sew a 1½″ × 13½″ background rectangle above the unit from Step 8 and press. Then sew a 1½″ × 15½″ background rectangle to the left side of the unit and press. Your block should measure 14½″ × 15½″. **Figure H**

10. Repeat Steps 1–9 to make 12 blocks for crib size, 20 for lap size, 30 for twin size, 36 for full/queen size, or 49 for king size.

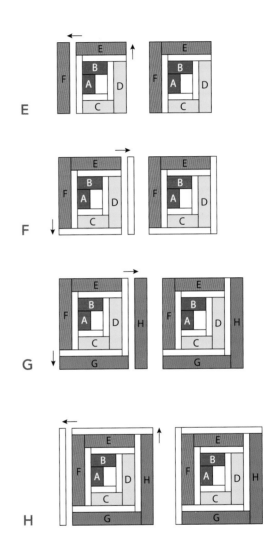

E

F

G

H

QUILT ASSEMBLY

1. Refer to the quilt assembly diagram (page 59) to arrange the blocks into horizontal rows according to the size you are making:

> **Crib:** 4 rows of 3 blocks
>
> **Lap:** 5 rows of 4 blocks
>
> **Twin:** 6 rows of 5 blocks
>
> **Full/queen:** 6 rows of 6 blocks
>
> **King:** 7 rows of 7 blocks

2. Sew the blocks together into rows. Press the seams in row 1 to the right, row 2 to the left, and so on.

3. Sew the rows together and press.

FINISHING

1. Layer the top, batting, and backing and quilt as desired.

2. Add the binding. (See General Instructions, page 14.)

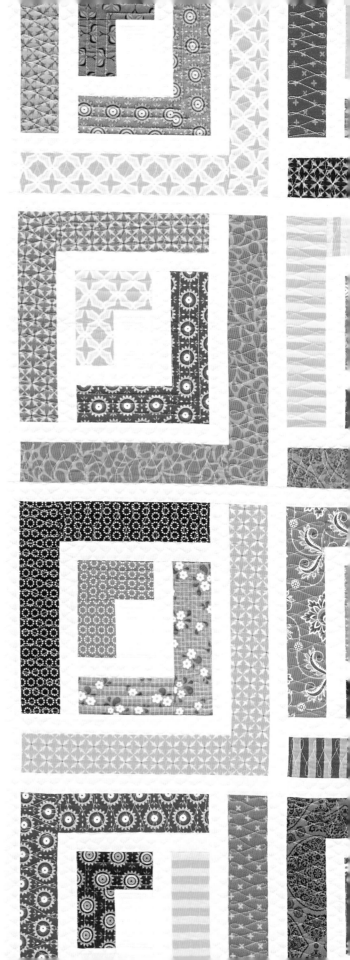

Lap size

Square Dance

Finished block: 14″ × 14″ or 17″ × 17″ (tilted) • **Quilt sizes:** crib, lap, twin/full, queen, king

Materials

MATERIALS	CRIB SIZE 38″ × 55″	LAP SIZE 55″ × 72″	TWIN/FULL SIZE 72″ × 89″	QUEEN SIZE 89″ × 106″	KING SIZE 106″ × 106″
2½″ × WOF* STRIPS	15	30	50	75	90
BACKGROUND FABRIC	1½ yards	2¾ yards	4¼ yards	6 yards	7 yards
BINDING FABRIC	½ yard	⅝ yard	¾ yard	⅞ yard	1 yard
BACKING FABRIC	2¾ yards	3⅝ yards	5½ yards	8 yards	9⅝ yards
BATTING	46″ × 63″	63″ × 80″	80″ × 97″	97″ × 114″	114″ × 114″

* WOF = width of fabric
Yardage based on 42″ width of fabric.

Cutting

MATERIALS	CRIB SIZE 6 BLOCKS	LAP SIZE 12 BLOCKS	TWIN/FULL SIZE 20 BLOCKS	QUEEN SIZE 30 BLOCKS	KING SIZE 36 BLOCKS
Assorted 2½″ × WOF strips for center block square	3	6	10	15	18
Cut each strip into:					
2½″ × 6½″ rectangles	4	4	4	4	4
2½″ × 2½″ squares	4	4	4	4	4
Assorted 2½″ × WOF strips for outside block squares	12	24	40	60	72
Cut each strip into:					
2½″ × 6½″ rectangles	2	2	2	2	2
2½″ × 4½″ rectangles	2	2	2	2	2
2½″ × 2½″ squares	4	4	4	4	4
BACKGROUND FABRIC					
Cut strips 2½″ × WOF.	5	10	16	23	28
Subcut into:					
2½″ × 4½″ rectangles	24	48	80	120	144
2½″ × 2½″ squares	30	60	100	150	180
Cut strips 4″ × WOF.	6	12	20	30	36
Subcut into 4″ × 18″ rectangles.	12	24	40	60	72
Cut strips 2½″ × WOF for borders.	5	7	8	10	11
BINDING FABRIC					
Cut strips 2½″ × WOF.	5	7	9	11	12

Square Dance, lap size. Sewn by Gudrun Erla, quilted by Teresa Silva.

Construction

Seam allowances are ¼″.

BLOCK ASSEMBLY

Follow the arrows for pressing direction.

Make the blocks

1. Choose 5 different fabrics for a block. You will need 2 squares 2½″ × 2½″ and 2 rectangles 2½″ × 6½″ of the same fabric for the center square (A). For the 4 outer partial squares (B, C, D, and E), you will need 4 different sets of 2 squares 2½″ × 2½″, 1 rectangle 2½″ × 4½″, and 1 rectangle 2½″ × 6½″ of the same color. **Figure A**

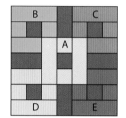

A

2. Sew a 2½″ × 2½″ background square between 2 A squares 2½″ × 2½″. Press. Repeat this step to make 1 unit for each fabric A–E. **Figure B**

B

3. Sew a 2½″ × 6½″ A rectangle to each side of the A unit from Step 2 to make the center square. Press. **Figure C**

C

4. Sew a 2½″ × 6½″ B rectangle to one side of the B unit from Step 1. Repeat this step with the remaining Step 1 units (C–E). **Figure D**

D

5. Sew a 2½″ × 4½″ background rectangle between a 2½″ × 4½″ B and D rectangle as shown. Press. Repeat this step with the C and E rectangles. Press. **Figure E**

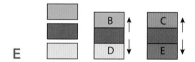

E

6. Sew the B/D and C/E units from Step 5 on each side of the A unit from Step 3, making sure the units are oriented exactly as shown. Press. Figure F

F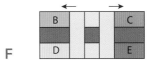

7. Sew the C and B units from Step 4 to the sides of a 2½″ × 4½″ background rectangle as shown. Press. Repeat this step with the D and E units from Step 4. Press. Figure G

G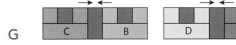

8. Sew the 2 units from Step 7 to the sides of the unit from Step 6, as shown. Press. Figure H

H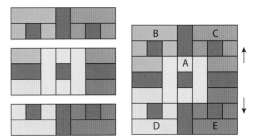

9. Repeat Steps 1–8 to make 6 blocks for crib size, 12 for lap size, 20 for twin/full size, 30 for queen size, or 36 for king size.

Tilting the blocks

1. Mark half of the 4″ × 18″ rectangles ¼″ from the bottom left corner and ¼″ from the top right corner. Use a ruler and a rotary cutter to cut the rectangles diagonally in half following the marks. Figure I

I

2. Repeat Step 1 to mark and cut the remaining rectangles in half diagonally in the *opposite* direction, from bottom right to top left. Figure J

J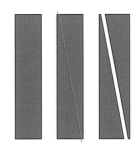

3. Using only the triangles cut in Step 1, add the triangles to the blocks with a partial seam method, working around the block counterclockwise. Layer a triangle on the right-hand side of a finished block, aligning the top right corners. Sew the triangle to the block, stopping about 2″ from the edge of the block. Press. Figure K

K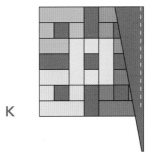

4. Layer a second triangle along the upper edge of the block as shown; sew the entire seam. Align the wide end of the triangle with the left-hand side of the block. Press outward. Figure L

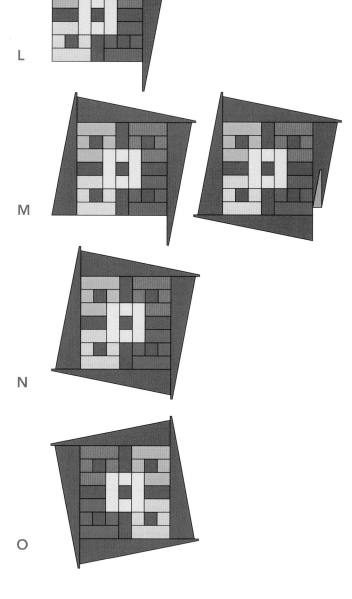

L

5. Repeat Step 4 to add the third and fourth triangles along the left side and bottom of the block. Fold the loose end of the first triangle out of the way. Press outward. Figure M

M

6. Unfold the first triangle and finish sewing that seam. Figure N

7. Repeat Steps 3–6 to make 3 blocks for crib size, 6 for lap size, 10 for twin/full size, 15 for queen size, or 18 for king size.

8. Repeat Steps 3–6 with the triangles cut in Step 2 and the remaining blocks, this time working around the block clockwise. Make the following mirror-image blocks tilted in the opposite direction: 3 blocks for crib size, 6 for lap size, 10 for twin/full size, 15 for queen size, or 18 for king size. Figure O

N

O

9. Trim all the blocks to 17½″ × 17½″, including seam allowances. Figure P

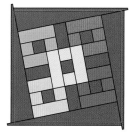
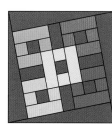
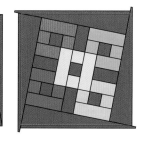
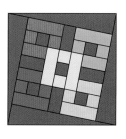

P

QUILT ASSEMBLY

1. Arrange the blocks into horizontal rows according to the size you are making:

> **Crib:** 3 rows of 2 blocks
>
> **Lap:** 3 rows of 4 blocks
>
> **Twin/full:** 4 rows of 5 blocks
>
> **Queen:** 5 rows of 6 blocks
>
> **King:** 6 rows of 6 blocks

As you arrange the blocks, alternate the direction of the tilted blocks as shown in the quilt assembly diagram (at right) to get the right effect.

2. Sew the blocks together into rows. Press the seams in row 1 to the right, row 2 to the left, and so on.

3. Sew the rows together and press.

BORDERS

Sew the 2½˝ border strips together into a long strip and attach it to the quilt. (See Borders, page 14.)

FINISHING

1. Layer the top, batting, and backing and quilt as desired.

2. Add the binding. (See General Instructions, page 14.)

Quilt assembly, lap size

Ripple Effect

Finished block: 12″ × 16″ • **Quilt sizes:** crib, lap, twin, full, queen, king

Materials

MATERIALS	CRIB SIZE 36″ × 48″	LAP SIZE 60″ × 80″	TWIN SIZE 60″ × 96″	FULL SIZE 72″ × 96″	QUEEN SIZE 84″ × 96″	KING SIZE 108″ × 112″
2½″ × WOF* STRIPS	9	25	30	36	42	63
BACKGROUND FABRIC	1⅜ yards	3½ yards	4⅛ yards	4⅞ yards	5¾ yards	8½ yards
BINDING	½ yard	⅝ yard	¾ yard	¾ yard	⅞ yard	1 yard
BACKING	1½ yards (2⅝ yards if fabric is less than 44″ wide)	4 yards (5 yards if fabric is less than 44″ wide)	6 yards	6 yards	7⅞ yards	9⅞ yards
BATTING	44″ × 56″	68″ × 88″	68″ × 104″	80″ × 104″	92″ × 104″	116″ × 120″

* WOF = width of fabric

Yardage based on 42″ width of fabric, except for crib and lap size backings.

Cutting

MATERIALS	CRIB SIZE 9 BLOCKS	LAP SIZE 25 BLOCKS	TWIN SIZE 30 BLOCKS	FULL SIZE 36 BLOCKS	QUEEN SIZE 42 BLOCKS	KING SIZE 63 BLOCKS
BACKGROUND FABRIC						
Cut strips 2½˝ × WOF for strip sets.	9	25	30	36	42	63
Cut strips 2½˝ × WOF.	8	23	27	32	38	56
Subcut into rectangles:						
2½˝ × 6½˝	36	100	120	144	168	252
2½˝ × 4½˝	18	50	60	72	84	126
BINDING FABRIC						
Cut strips 2½˝ × WOF.	5	8	9	9	10	12

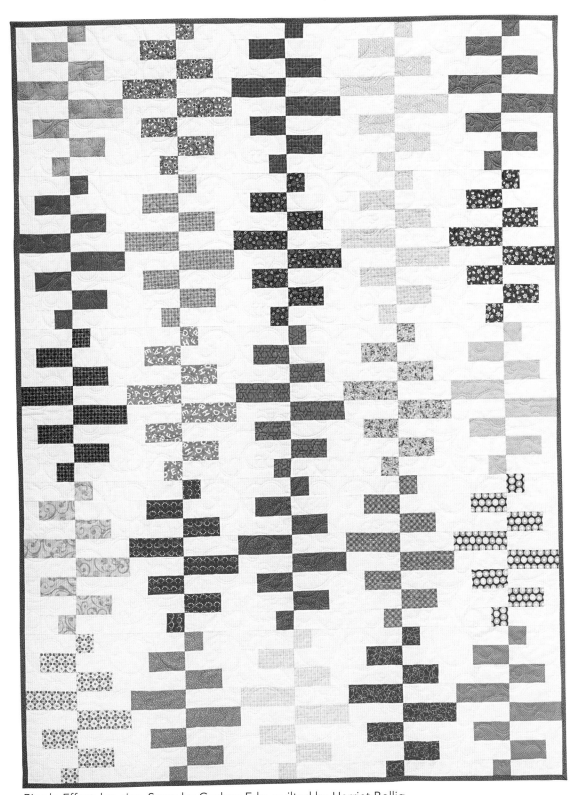

Ripple Effect, lap size. Sewn by Gudrun Erla, quilted by Harriet Bollig.

Construction

Seam allowances are ¼˝.

BLOCK ASSEMBLY

Follow the arrows for pressing direction.

Make the strip sets

1. Sew a 2½˝ × width of fabric colored strip to a 2½˝ × width of fabric background strip. Press toward the colored fabric. Each strip set will make 1 block. Make 9 strip sets for crib size, 25 for lap size, 30 for twin size, 36 for full size, 42 for queen size, and 63 for king size. **Figure A**

2. Cut each of the strip sets from Step 1 into 2 units 6½˝ wide, 4 units 4½˝ wide, and 2 units 2½˝ wide. Group the units with the same fabrics together to stay organized. **Figure B**

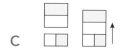

Make the blocks

1. Sew a 2½˝-wide strip set unit below a 4½˝-wide strip set unit of the same color and press. Repeat this step to make 2 from each strip set. **Figure C**

2. Sew a 2½˝ × 6½˝ background rectangle to the left side of the Step 1 unit as shown and press. Repeat this step to make 2 from each strip set. **Figure D**

3. Sew a 2½˝ × 4½˝ background rectangle to the right side of a 4½˝-wide strip set unit as shown and press. Repeat this step to make 2 from each strip set. **Figure E**

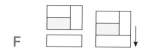

4. Sew a 2½˝ × 6½˝ background rectangle to the bottom of the Step 3 unit as shown and press. Repeat this step to make 2 from each strip set. **Figure F**

5. Sew a 6½˝-wide strip set unit between a unit from Step 2 and a unit from Step 4, making sure to orient all the units as shown. Press according to the arrows. Repeat this step to make 2 from each strip set. `Figure G`

6. Rotate a Step 5 unit 180°, and then sew both units together as shown. Press. Repeat this step to make 9 blocks for crib size, 25 for lap size, 30 for twin size, 36 for full size, 42 for queen size, and 63 for king size. Your blocks should measure 12½˝ × 16½˝. `Figure H`

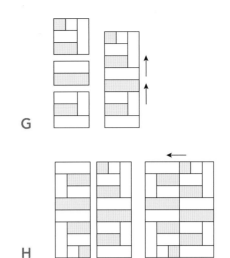

G

H

QUILT ASSEMBLY

1. Arrange the blocks into rows according to the size you are making:

> **Crib:** 3 rows of 3 blocks
>
> **Lap:** 5 rows of 5 blocks
>
> **Twin:** 5 rows of 6 blocks
>
> **Full:** 6 rows of 6 blocks
>
> **Queen:** 7 rows of 6 blocks
>
> **King:** 9 rows of 7 blocks

As you arrange the blocks, make sure that the center seam of all the blocks in row 1 are pressed to the right, to the left in row 2, and so on. (Just rotate the blocks 180° to get all the seam allowances facing the correct way.)

2. Sew the blocks together into rows. Press the seams in row 1 to the right, row 2 to the left, and so on.

3. Sew the rows together and press.

Quilt assembly, lap size

FINISHING

1. Layer the top, batting, and backing and quilt as desired.

2. Add the binding. (See General Instructions, page 14.)

Ribbon Candy

Finished block: 12″ × 12″ • **Quilt sizes:** crib, lap, full, king

Materials

MATERIALS	CRIB SIZE 44″ × 61″	LAP SIZE 61″ × 78″	FULL SIZE 78″ × 95″	KING SIZE 101″ × 101″
2½″ × WOF* STRIPS	8	18	32	41
BACKGROUND FABRIC	⅞ yard	1¾ yards	3 yards	3¾ yards
NARROW BORDER FABRIC	¼ yard	⅜ yard	½ yard	¾ yard
WIDE BORDER FABRIC	1⅔ yards	2¼ yards	2⅔ yards	3½ yards
BINDING	½ yard	⅝ yard	⅞ yard	⅞ yard
BACKING	3 yards	5 yards	7⅓ yards	9¼ yards
BATTING	52″ × 69″	69″ × 86″	86″ × 103″	109″ × 109″

* WOF = width of fabric

Yardage based on 42″ width of fabric.

Cutting

MATERIALS	CRIB SIZE 8 BLOCKS	LAP SIZE 18 BLOCKS	FULL SIZE 32 BLOCKS	KING SIZE 41 BLOCKS
2½″ × WOF STRIPS	Cut the following from each strip:			
2½″ × 6½″ rectangles	4	4	4	4
2½″ × 2½″ squares	2	2	2	2

CUTTING continued on next page

MATERIALS	CRIB SIZE 8 BLOCKS	LAP SIZE 18 BLOCKS	FULL SIZE 32 BLOCKS	KING SIZE 41 BLOCKS
BACKGROUND FABRIC				
Cut strips 4½˝ × WOF.	4	8	15	19
Subcut into rectangles: 4½˝ × 6½˝	16	36	64	82
4½˝ × 2½˝	16	36	64	82
Cut strips 2½˝ × WOF.	3	7	12	16
Subcut into 2½˝ × 2½˝ squares.	48	108	192	246
NARROW BORDER FABRIC				
Cut strips 1½˝ × WOF.	5	7	8	
Cut strips 2½˝ × WOF.				9
SETTING TRIANGLES AND WIDE BORDER FABRIC				
Cut 18¼˝ × 18¼˝ squares. Cut each twice diagonally to make side setting triangles.	2 (8 triangles; you will use 6)	3 (12 triangles; you will use 10)	4 (16 triangles; you will use 14)	4 (16 triangles)
Cut 9½˝ × 9½˝ squares. Cut each once diagonally to make corner setting triangles.	2 (4 triangles)	2 (4 triangles)	2 (4 triangles)	2 (4 triangles)
Cut strips 4½˝ × WOF.	6	8	9	
Cut strips 6½˝ × WOF.				11
BINDING FABRIC				
Cut strips 2½˝ × WOF.	6	8	10	11

Ribbon Candy, lap size. Sewn by Yvonne Geske, quilted by Harriet Bollig.

Construction

Seam allowances are ¼".

BLOCK ASSEMBLY

Follow the arrows for pressing direction.

Make the blocks

1. Pick 2 rectangles 2½" × 6½" and a 2½" × 2½" square each from 2 different 2½" × width of fabric strips. (They can be a light and a dark of the same hue, like mine, or 2 different colors. Call these color 1 and color 2.) Sew a 2½" × 2½" background square on each side of the 2½" × 2½" squares from colors 1 and 2. Press. **Figure A**

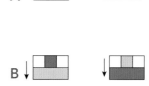

2. Sew a 2½" × 6½" color 2 rectangle to the color 1 unit from Step 1 and press. Sew a 2½" × 6½" color 1 rectangle to the color 2 unit from Step 1 and press. **Figure B**

3. Sew a 2½" × 4½" background rectangle to the right side of both units from Step 2. Press. **Figure C**

4. Sew a 2½" × 2½" background square to the 2½" × 6½" rectangles from colors 1 and 2. Press. **Figure D**

5. Sew the units from Step 4 below the units from Step 3, oriented exactly as shown. Press. **Figure E**

6. Sew a 4½" × 6½" background rectangle to the right side of both units from Step 5. Press. **Figure F**

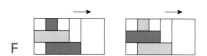

7. Sew the units from Step 6 together into a block and press. Your block should measure 12½" × 12½". **Figure G**

8. Repeat Steps 1–7 to make a total of 8 blocks for crib size, 18 for lap size, 32 for full size, and 41 for king size.

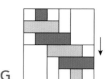

QUILT ASSEMBLY

1. Follow the quilt assembly diagrams to arrange the blocks on point into diagonal rows according to the size you are making:

> **Crib:** 3 rows of 2 blocks with 2 rows of 1 block in between
>
> **Lap:** 4 rows of 3 blocks with 3 rows of 2 blocks in between
>
> **Full:** 5 rows of 4 blocks with 4 rows of 3 blocks in between
>
> **King:** 5 rows of 5 blocks with 4 rows of 4 blocks in between

Add the setting triangles and corner triangles to your layout.

2. Sew the blocks and triangles together into diagonal rows. Press the seams in row 1 to the right, row 2 to the left, row 3 to the right, and so on.

3. Sew the rows together and press.

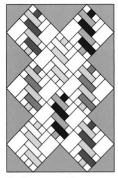

Quilt assembly, crib size

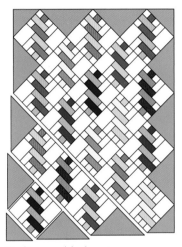

Quilt assembly, lap size

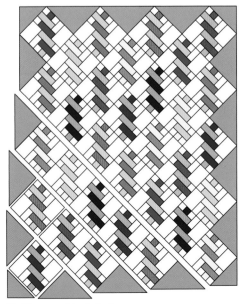

Quilt assembly, full size

Quilt assembly, king size

BORDERS

1. Sew the narrow border strips together into a long strip and attach it to the quilt. (See Borders, page 14.)

2. Repeat Step 1 with the wide border strips.

FINISHING

1. Layer the top, batting, and backing and quilt as desired.

2. Add the binding. (See General Instructions, page 14.)

Borders, full size

SCRAP CRAZIES

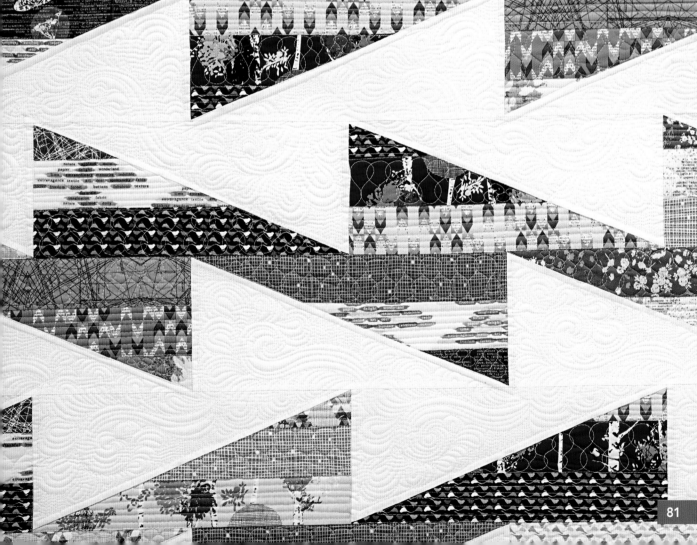

Pebbles

Finished block: 14″ × 14″ • **Quilt sizes:** lap, twin

Materials

MATERIALS	LAP SIZE 56″ × 56″	TWIN SIZE 56″ × 84″
2½″ × WOF* STRIPS	40	60
BACKGROUND FABRIC	¾ yard	1½ yards
BINDING	½ yard	⅝ yard
BACKING	3¾ yards	5¼ yards
BATTING	64″ × 64″	64″ × 92″

* WOF = width of fabric
Yardage based on 42″ width of fabric.

Cutting

MATERIALS	LAP SIZE 16 BLOCKS	TWIN SIZE 24 BLOCKS
BACKGROUND FABRIC		
Cut strips 1½″ × WOF.	1	2
Cut strips 2½″ × WOF.	1	2
Cut strips 3½″ × WOF.	1	2
Cut strips 4½″ × WOF.	1	2
Cut strips 5½″ × WOF.	1	2
Cut strips 6½″ × WOF.	1	2
BINDING		
Cut strips 2½″ × WOF.	6	8

Pebbles, lap size. Sewn by Gudrun Erla, quilted by Harriet Bollig.

Construction

Seam allowances are ¼˝.

BLOCK ASSEMBLY

Follow the arrows for pressing direction.

Make the strip sets

1. If you are making the twin size quilt, cut 20 of the assorted 2½˝ × width of fabric strips in half on the center fold so they measure about 21˝; you will be making some half strip sets.

2. Make strip set A by sewing together 7 of the 2½˝-wide strips along the long edges. Press. Make 1 full strip set for lap size or 1 full and 1 half strip set for twin size. Subcut the strip sets into 2½˝-wide strips; you will need 16 for lap size or 24 for twin size. Figure A

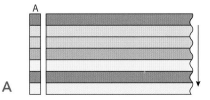

A

3. Make strip set B by sewing together 7 of the 2½˝-wide strips and a 1½˝-wide background strip at the top. Press. Make 1 full strip set for lap size or 1 full and 1 half strip set for twin size. Subcut the strip set into 2½˝-wide strips; you will need 16 for lap size or 24 for twin size. Figure B

B

4. Make strip set C by sewing together 6 of the 2½˝-wide strips and a 2½˝-wide background strip at the top. Press. Make 1 full strip set for lap size or 1 full and 1 half strip set for twin size. Subcut the strip sets into 2½˝-wide strips; you will need 16 for lap size or 24 for twin size. Figure C

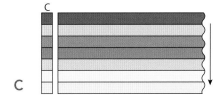

C

5. Make strip set D by sewing together 6 of the 2½˝-wide strips and a 3½˝-wide background strip at the top. Press. Make 1 full strip set for lap size or 1 full and 1 half strip set for twin size. Subcut the strip sets into 2½˝-wide strips; you will need 16 for lap size or 24 for twin size. Figure D

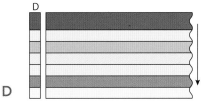

D

6. Make strip set E by sewing together 5 of the 2½˝ assorted strips and a 4½˝-wide background strip. Press. Make 1 full strip set for lap size or 1 full and 1 half strip set for twin size. Subcut the strip sets into 2½˝-wide strips; you will need 16 for lap size or 24 for twin size. Figure E

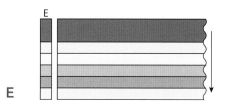

7. Make strip set F by sewing together 5 of the 2½˝ assorted strips and a 5½˝-wide background strip. Press. Make 1 full strip set for lap size or 1 full and 1 half strip set for twin size. Subcut the strip sets into 2½˝-wide strips; you will need 16 for lap size or 24 for twin size. Figure F

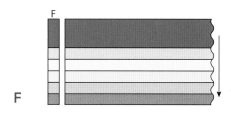

8. Make strip set G by sewing together 4 of the 2½˝ assorted strips and a 6½˝-wide background strip. Press. Make 1 full strip set for lap size or 1 full and 1 half strip set for twin size. Subcut the strip sets into 2½˝-wide strips; you will need 16 for lap size or 24 for twin size. Figure G

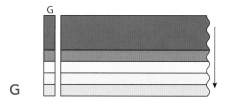

Make the blocks

1. Each block is put together with 1 each of strip units A–G. Arrange them in order as shown and sew them together by aligning the top (background fabric) edges. Press. Figure H

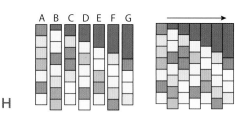

2. Repeat Step 1 to make 16 blocks for lap size or 24 for twin size. Trim the excess pieces off the bottom of the blocks as shown so the blocks measure 14½˝ × 14½˝, including seam allowances. Figure I

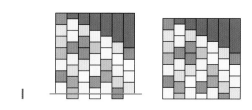

QUILT ASSEMBLY

1. Follow the quilt assembly diagram (at right) to arrange the blocks into rows, rotating blocks so the backgrounds meet, according to the size you are making:

> **Lap:** 4 rows of 4 blocks
>
> **Twin:** 6 rows of 4 blocks

2. Sew the blocks into rows. Press the seams in row 1 to the right, row 2 to the left, and so on.

3. Sew the rows together and press.

FINISHING

1. Layer the top, batting, and backing and quilt as desired.

2. Add the binding. (See General Instructions, page 14.)

Quilt assembly, lap size

Pixel Wheels

Finished block: 24″ × 24″ • **Quilt sizes:** lap, queen

Materials

MATERIALS	LAP SIZE 72″ × 72″	QUEEN SIZE 96″ × 96″
2½″ × WOF* STRIPS	13	20
BACKGROUND FABRIC	4¾ yards	8¼ yards
BINDING	⅝ yard	¾ yard
BACKING	4⅝ yards	8⅞ yards
BATTING	80″ × 80″	104″ × 104″

* WOF = width of fabric

Yardage based on 42″ width of fabric.

Cutting

MATERIALS	LAP SIZE 9 BLOCKS	QUEEN SIZE 16 BLOCKS
BACKGROUND FABRIC		
Cut strips 4½″ × WOF for strip piecing.	3	4
Cut strips 2½″ × WOF for strip piecing.	8	12
Cut strips 1½″ × WOF for strip piecing.	10	16
Cut strips 12½″ × WOF.	4	8
Subcut into 12½″ × 4½″ rectangles.	36	64
Cut strips 8½″ × WOF.	8	13
Subcut into rectangles: 8½″ × 2½″ 8½″ × 1½″	 72 72	 128 128
BINDING		
Cut strips 2½″ × WOF.	8	10

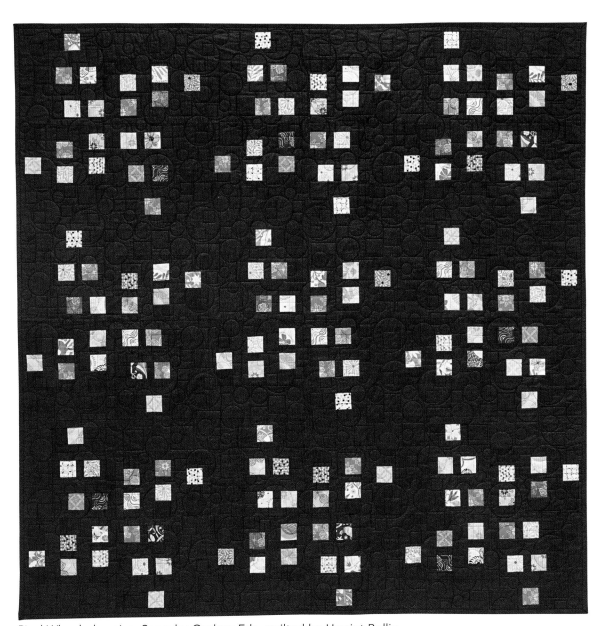

Pixel Wheels, lap size. Sewn by Gudrun Erla, quilted by Harriet Bollig.

Construction

Seam allowances are ¼″.

BLOCK ASSEMBLY

Follow the arrows for pressing direction.

Make the strip sets

1. Sew a background 4½″ × width of fabric strip to one side of a 2½″ × width of fabric assorted-colored strip. Then sew a background 2½″ × width of fabric strip to the other side of the colored strip to make strip set A. Press. Repeat this step to make 3 A strip sets for lap size or 4 for queen size. Subcut the strip sets into 2½″-wide units. You will need 36 for lap size or 64 for queen size. **Figure A**

A

2. Sew together a background 2½″ × width of fabric strip, 2 different colors of 2½″ × width of fabric strips, and 2 background 1½″ × width of fabric strips as shown to make strip set B. Repeat this step to make 5 B strip sets for lap size or 8 for queen size. Subcut the strip sets into 2½″-wide units. You will need 72 for lap size or 128 for queen size. **Figure B**

B

C

Make the blocks

1. Sew an A strip unit, 2 background 2½″ × 8½″ rectangles, 2 B strip units, and 2 background 1½″ × 8½″ rectangles together as shown. Make sure to orient the units exactly as shown. Press. Repeat this step to make 36 units for lap size or 64 for queen size. **Figure C**

D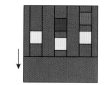

2. Sew a background 4½″ × 12½″ rectangle to the block units from Step 1 as shown to make quarter-block units. Press. **Figure D**

3. Sew all the quarter-block units together in pairs as shown, rotating 1 unit 90° clockwise. Press. Sew the pairs into blocks, rotating 1 pair 180° as shown. Press the left and right sides of the last seam in opposite directions, removing a few stitches as needed from the center of the last seam so the center seam intersection lays flat.

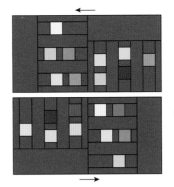
E
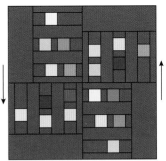

Figure E

QUILT ASSEMBLY

1. Arrange the blocks into horizontal rows according to the size you are making:

> **Lap:** 3 rows of 3 blocks
>
> **Queen:** 4 rows of 4 blocks

2. Sew the blocks together into rows. Press the seams in row 1 to the right, row 2 to the left, and so on.

3. Sew the rows together and press.

FINISHING

1. Layer the top, batting, and backing and quilt as desired.

2. Add the binding. (See General Instructions, page 14.)

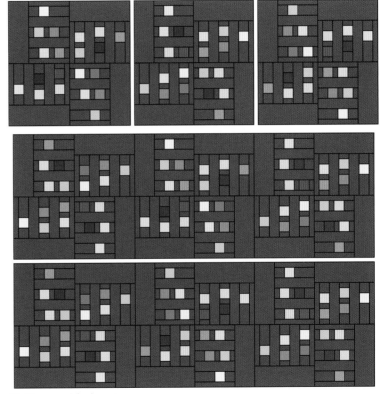

Quilt assembly, lap size

Bob and Weave

Finished block: 13˝ × 6˝ • Quilt sizes: crib, lap, full, queen

Materials

MATERIALS	CRIB SIZE 39″ × 48″	LAP SIZE 52″ × 72″	FULL SIZE 78″ × 96″	QUEEN SIZE 91″ × 96″
2½″ × WOF* STRIPS	12	24	48	57
BACKGROUND FABRIC	⅞ yard	1¾ yards	3⅛ yards	3⅝ yards
BINDING	½ yard	⅝ yard	¾ yard	⅞ yard
BACKING	2¾ yards	3½ yards	7⅓ yards	8⅜ yards
BATTING	47″ × 56″	60″ × 80″	86″ × 104″	99″ × 104″

* WOF = width of fabric

Yardage based on 42″ width of fabric.

Cutting

MATERIALS	CRIB SIZE 24 BLOCKS	LAP SIZE 48 BLOCKS	FULL SIZE 96 BLOCKS	QUEEN SIZE 30 BLOCKS
BACKGROUND FABRIC				
Cut strips 6½˝ × WOF.	4	8	16	19
Subcut into 6½˝ × 13½˝ rectangles.	12	24	48	56
BINDING FABRIC				
Cut strips 2½˝ × WOF.	5	7	9	10

Bob and Weave, lap size. Sewn by Gudrun Erla, quilted by Angela Walters.

Construction

Seam allowances are ¼˝.

BLOCK ASSEMBLY

Follow the arrows for pressing direction.

Make the strip sets

1. Sew together 3 different 2½˝ × width of fabric strips along the long edges. Press. Repeat this step to make a total of 4 strip sets for crib size, 8 for lap size, 16 for full size, or 19 for queen size. Figure A

2. Subcut each strip set into 3 rectangles 6½˝ × 13½˝ for a total of 12 for crib size, 24 for lap size, 48 for full size, or 57 for queen size (you will only use 56 for queen size). Figure B

3. Divide the strip set rectangles into 2 equal groups. Mark the first group of rectangles on the short sides ½˝ from the bottom left corner and ½˝ from the top right corner as shown. Line up a ruler on the marks and cut the strip units into triangles. These are the A triangles. Figure C

4. Repeat Step 3 to mark and cut half of the 6½˝ × 13½˝ background rectangles. Figure D

5. Repeat Step 3 to mark and cut mirror-image triangles with the remaining strip set and background rectangles—mark ½˝ from the top left corner and ½˝ from the bottom right corner. These are the B triangles. Figure E

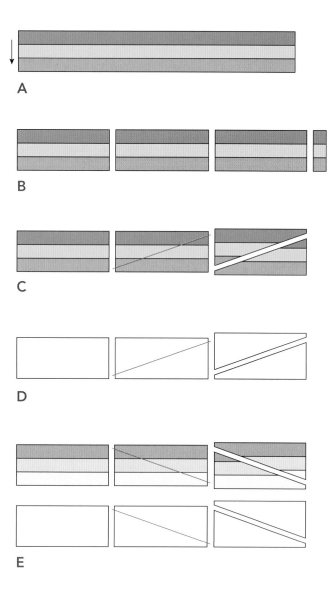

A

B

C

D

E

Make the blocks

1. Sew together a background A triangle and a strip set A triangle to make a block. Press toward the background. Repeat this step to make a total of 12 A blocks for crib size, 24 for lap size, 48 for full size, or 56 for queen size. **Figure F**

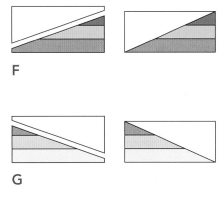

F

G

2. Sew together a background B triangle and a strip set B triangle. Press toward the background. The B blocks should be a mirror image of the A blocks. Repeat this step to make a total of 12 B blocks for crib size, 24 for lap size, 48 for full size, or 56 for queen size. **Figure G**

QUILT ASSEMBLY

1. Arrange the blocks into rows according to the size you are making, oriented exactly as shown in the initial row arrangement (below). The first 2 rows are all A blocks, the next 2 rows are all B blocks, and so on. *Note: Do not sew any blocks together yet.*

2. After you have arranged the blocks into rows and are happy with the color layout, remove the block that is farthest to the right in every even row. Cut these blocks in half vertically to make 2 half blocks 6½″ × 6¾″.

Crib: 8 rows of 3 blocks

Lap: 12 rows of 4 blocks

Full: 16 rows of 6 blocks

Queen: 16 rows of 7 blocks

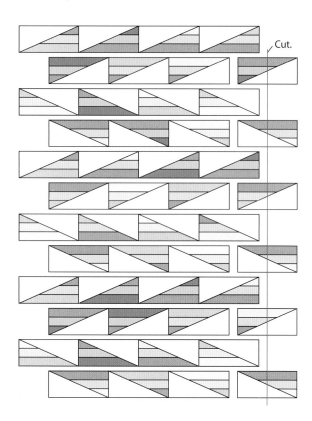

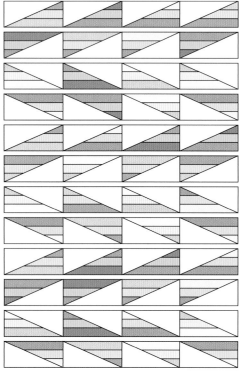

Initial row arrangement, lap size

3. Place the right-hand end of the half-block at the left side of the even row it was originally in, and move all the blocks in the row to the right. Fill in the empty space at the end of each even row with the half-block that was originally there.

4. Sew the blocks into rows. Press the seams in row 1 to the right, row 2 to the left, and so on.

5. The even rows will be ½″ shorter than the odd rows. Sew the rows together, making sure to center the shorter even rows on the odd rows (¼″ extending on each side). Press.

6. Trim the quilt so it is even on both sides.

Half-block from right

FINISHING

1. Layer the top, batting, and backing and quilt as desired.

2. Add the binding. (See General Instructions, page 14.)

Hang Glide

Finished block: 15½″ × 15½″ • **Quilt sizes:** crib, lap, twin/full, queen

Materials

MATERIALS	CRIB SIZE 37″ × 54½″	LAP SIZE 54½″ × 72″	TWIN/FULL SIZE 72″ × 89½″	QUEEN SIZE 89½″ × 89½″
2½″ × WOF* STRIPS** (NEUTRAL)	20	40	70	90
BLOCK SASHING FABRIC (RED)	½ yard	⅞ yard	1¼ yards	1½ yards
CORNERSTONE FABRIC (GRAY)	¼ yard	¼ yard	⅓ yard	⅓ yard
SASHING FABRIC (AQUA)***	⅔ yard	1 yard	1½ yards	2 yards
BINDING	½ yard	⅝ yard	¾ yard	⅞ yard
BACKING	2⅝ yards	3⅝ yards	5⅝ yards	8⅓ yards
BATTING	45″ × 63″	63″ × 80″	80″ × 98″	98″ × 98″

* WOF = width of fabric

Yardage based on 42″ width of fabric.

** You can use 2½″-wide strips cut from fat quarters, but you will need three times
the number of strips listed in the materials chart.

*** Fabric with a directional design may require additional yardage.

Tools needed: Either a 90° quarter-square ruler (I recommend CGRT90 from Creative Grids) or template plastic to trace and cut out the template.

Cutting

MATERIALS	CRIB SIZE 6 BLOCKS	LAP SIZE 12 BLOCKS	TWIN/FULL SIZE 20 BLOCKS	QUEEN SIZE 25 BLOCKS
BLOCK SASHING FABRIC				
Cut strips 2½˝ × WOF.	5	10	16	20
Subcut into 2½˝ × 7¼˝ rectangles.	24	48	80	100
CORNERSTONE FABRIC				
Cut strips 2½˝ × WOF.	2	2	4	4
Subcut into 2½˝ × 2½˝ squares.	18	32	50	61
SASHING FABRIC				
Cut strips 16˝ × WOF.	1	2	3	4
Subcut into 16˝ × 2½˝ rectangles.	16	31	48	60
Cut strips 2½˝ × WOF.	1		1	
Subcut into 2½˝ × 16˝ rectangles.	1		1	
BINDING				
Cut strips 2½˝ × WOF.	5	7	9	10

Hang Glide, lap size. Sewn by Gudrun Erla, quilted by Harriet Bollig.

Construction

Seam allowances are ¼˝.

BLOCK ASSEMBLY

Follow the arrows for pressing direction.

Make the strip sets

1. Sew together 3 neutral 2½˝ × width of fabric strips along the long edges to make a strip set. Press. Repeat this step to make 2 strip sets for crib size, 4 for lap size, 7 for twin/full size, or 9 for queen size. Figure A

2. Cut all the strip sets from Step 1 in half lengthwise, directly through the center strip. Sew another neutral 2½˝ × width of fabric strip to each side that was just cut to make the A strip sets. There should now be 4 A strip sets for crib size, 8 for lap size, 14 for twin/full size, or 18 for queen size. Press. Figure B

3. Sew together 5 neutral 2½˝ × width of fabric strips along the long edges to make a strip set. Press. Repeat this step to make 2 strip sets for crib size, 4 for lap size, 7 for full size, or 9 for queen size. Figure C

4. Cut all of the strip sets from Step 3 in half lengthwise, directly through the center strip, to make the B strip sets. There should now be 4 B strip sets for crib size, 8 for lap size, 14 for twin/full size, or 18 for queen size. Figure D

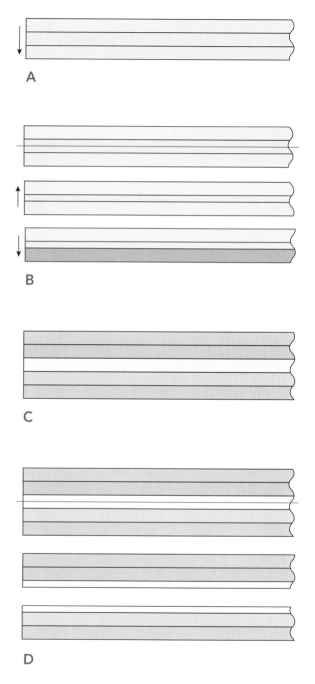

A

B

C

D

5. If you are not using a quarter-square triangle ruler, trace the pattern (page 109) for the triangle template onto template plastic and cut out. Using either the template or the triangle ruler, cut the A and B strip sets into triangles. Discard the end triangles. Keep the 2 groups separate. Figure E

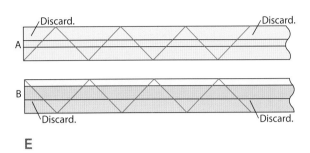

E

Make the blocks

1. Sew together an A triangle and a B triangle along the long sides. Press. The unit should measure 7¼″ × 7¼″ unfinished. Repeat this step to make a total of 24 A/B units for crib size, 48 for lap size, 80 for twin/full size, or 100 for queen size. Figure F

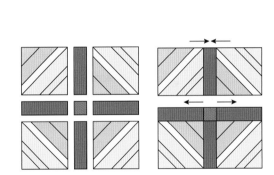

F

2. Lay out the block in 3 rows, each containing 4 A/B units, 1 cornerstone, and 4 block sashing 2½″ × 7¼″ rectangles as shown. Make sure that the A/B units are oriented as shown. Sew an A/B unit to each side of 2 block sashing rectangles and press. Sew the remaining 2 sashing rectangles to 2 opposite sides of the cornerstone and press. Sew all 3 rows together and press. The block should measure 16″ × 16″, including seam allowances. Figure G

G

3. Repeat Step 2 to make a total of 6 blocks for crib size, 12 for lap size, 20 for twin/full size, or 25 for queen size.

QUILT ASSEMBLY

1. Refer to the quilt assembly diagram to arrange the blocks, the 2½″ × 16″ sashing strips, and the remaining cornerstones into rows, according to the size you are making:

> **Crib:** 3 rows of 2 blocks
>
> **Lap:** 4 rows of 3 blocks
>
> **Twin/full:** 5 rows of 4 blocks
>
> **Queen:** 5 rows of 5 blocks

2. Sew the blocks and vertical sashing strips together into rows. Sew the horizontal sashing strips and cornerstones into rows. Press all seams toward the sashing strips.

3. Sew all the rows together and press.

Quilt assembly, lap size

FINISHING

1. Layer the top, batting, and backing and quilt as desired.

2. Add the binding. (See General Instructions, page 14.)

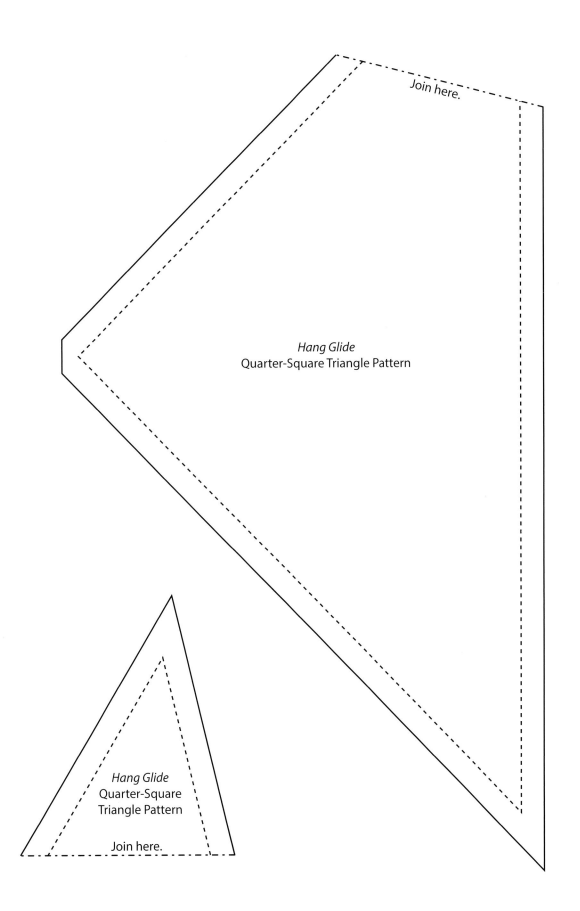

Hang Glide
Quarter-Square Triangle Pattern

Join here.

Hang Glide
Quarter-Square
Triangle Pattern

Join here.